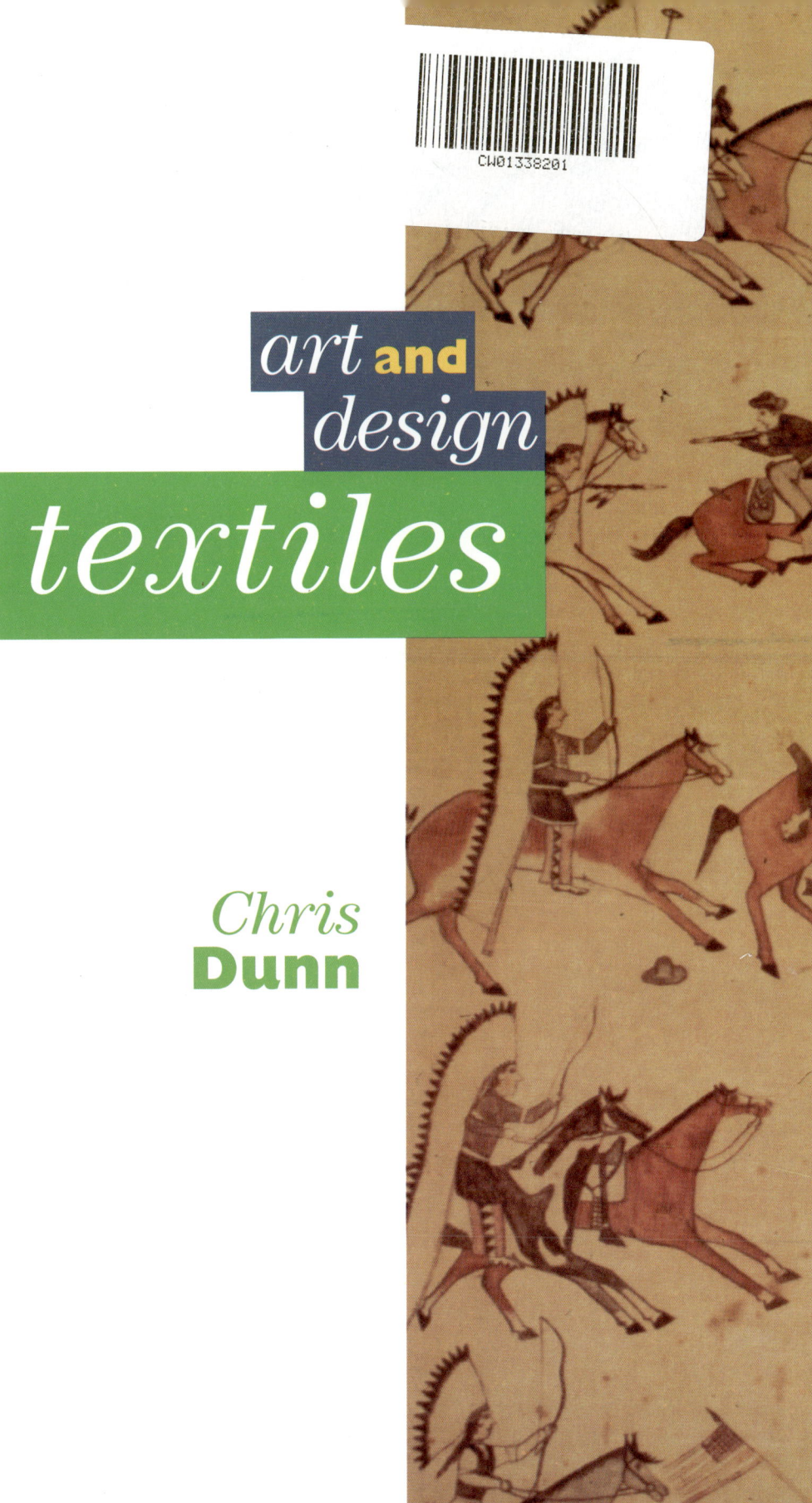

art and design
textiles

Chris **Dunn**

Hodder & Stoughton
A MEMBER OF THE HODDER HEADLINE GROUP

TEXTILES

Introduction

The Textiles syllabuses are designed to encourage as wide a use and understanding of textiles as possible. It is not, therefore, a narrowly skills based subject. As you will see from the wide range of samples collected in this book, the only limiting factor is the imagination of the artist. The degree of manipulation of the often traditional techniques, possible by an imaginative artist, is astounding. The traditional subject matter, the content, has expanded; an example of this is the use in advertising of soft sculpture techniques. The flexible use of materials, the form, has also undergone a radical transformation as can be seen in these students' works.

Student's work, kimono in coloured tissue, run through with threads. Life size.

ART & DESIGN

Student's work, half figure, on a foil base with various textiles. Life size.

Few of the demands of the creative artist cannot be encompassed within the highly flexible group of materials known as textiles. The two pieces of work by students pictured here show how non-traditional materials can be used. In the first, a kimono, the fabric is held together with a series of threads onto which bright tissue paper has been built. The whole piece is reinforced by the glue used. The bodice was built onto a foil form which was pressed onto a costume dummy. It was then cut away and reinforced with layers of thin, white paper. It has kept the body shape and has been decorated with lace, bows and folds of near-white cloth. Gold thread, painted flowers and poetry written in gold complete the decoration.

The inspiration for these two pieces comes from two very different cultures – Japan and Elizabethan England. Their translation into modern media illustrates an intelligent interpretation of those cultures and an open, creative mind in their translation.

These examples of students' work show how creatively the two attainment targets of Investigating and Making, and Knowledge and Understanding can be achieved within the context of textiles.

TEXTILES

Looking at Textiles

The *Anteater* embroidery below with its bright colours on a black background, loose threads and open stitching shows that freedom from precision and craft skills are not necessarily a bad thing. To get true value from your work you must be prepared to break through the restrictions that traditional techniques often impose. It is important that these skills are learnt, for in this way the quality of what you aim to produce will improve. Skills, however well developed, will not replace the imagination of the artist but they can enhance the way your work is carried out. Above all they should be regarded as a means to an end rather than the end in itself.

Jeanne Abell, Anteater, *embroidery. (Photograph by Richard Abell).*

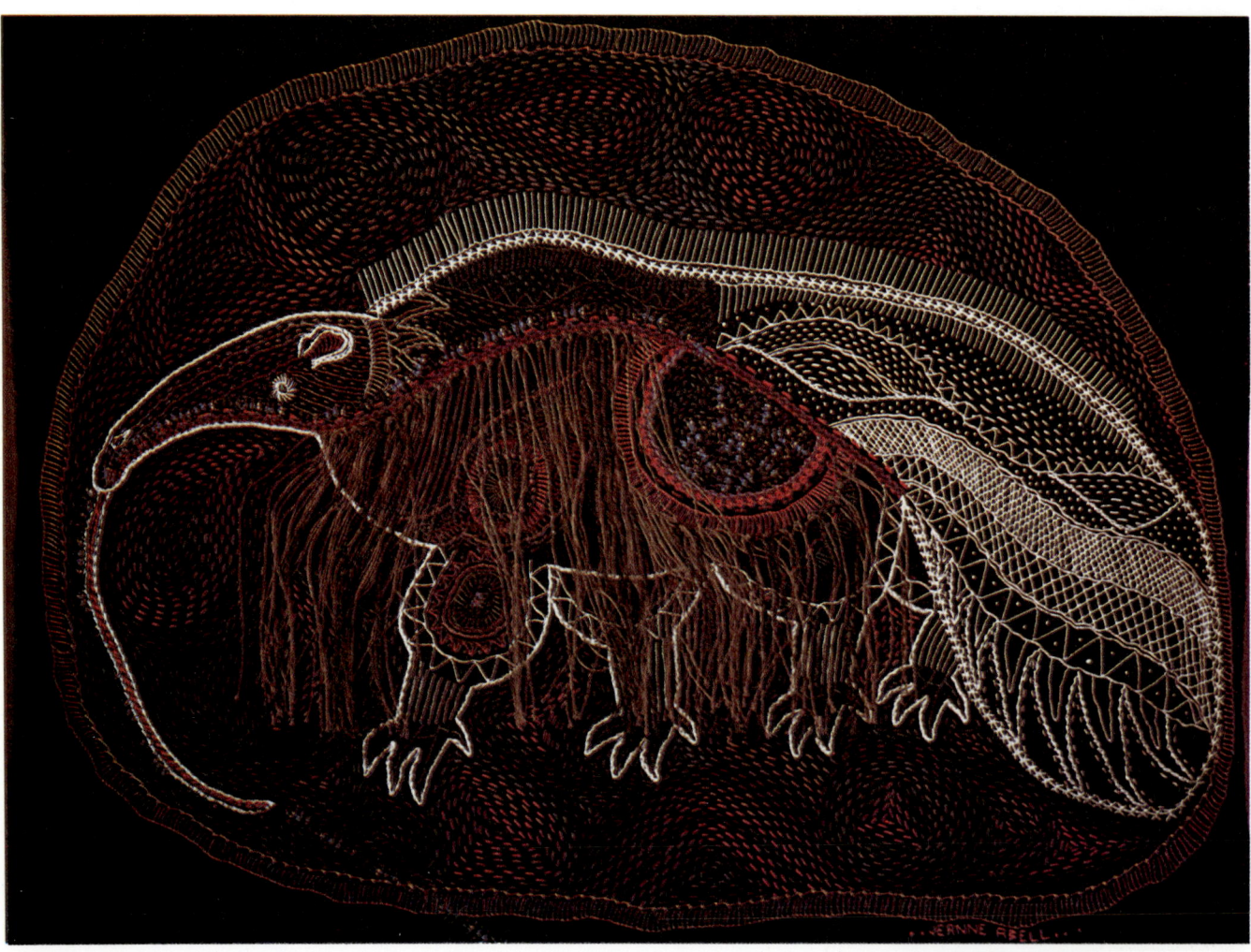

Jennie Parry, The Golden Apple of the Hesperides, *papier mâché and embroidery.*

Curtis and Suzanne Benzle, Willow Weep 2, *porcelain bowl, 18 cm diameter.*

Student's bowl, papier mâché.

This book will not stress the technical aspects of the subject. You will find many technical textbooks are available if you feel you need them or you could take advantage of the most useful resource of all, your teacher's knowledge. Here we will try to develop a flexible, progressive way of looking at textiles and from this insight your own vision may develop. Contrast the effect of this porcelain piece, made from two different coloured clays blended together with this piece (above) by Jennie Parry. This piece is made from papier mâché, formed over an apple. It has then been covered with fabric and embroidered in gold thread. The lacey leaf shapes are built on wire foundations. You might like to try embroidery on similar three-dimensional forms, perhaps built of papier mâché as well but in the form of open bowls. You can do this by moulding round the bowl. The student has used coloured tissue moulded around a low dish or plate to create this colourful form (right).

They demonstrate that textiles can be formed in ways that rival other materials and add dimensions that other materials cannot imitate. The imaginative artist often tries to stretch the frontiers of the materials they use and it is often along these frontiers that the most interesting, and risky, work appears.

These two examples illustrate two of the basic divisions within the overall 'Textiles' heading: those fabrics that are made or constructed and those that are decorated or coloured. Naturally, as we see throughout this series, clear cut boundaries defining the use of materials are there only as a guide and they are meant to be challenged. Woven cloth is often decorated, while decoration needs a basic support to hold it together, even if the embroidered support is dissolved afterwards to leave just the embroidery.

ART & DESIGN 5

Textiles

Franco-Flemish tapestry, The Pheasant Hunt, *wool and silk, 317.5 × 327.5 cm, Burrell Collection, Glasgow.*

Objects that have been woven, knitted or felted can be grouped under the heading 'constructed textiles'. Tapestry and lace can also be said to be constructed. Though they are usually too complex to be attempted in school, they provide creative examples from the past. Decorated textiles can be embroidered or they can be coloured by printing and dying. Textiles are the most physically flexible of media. They move, fold and crease with ease. Textile designers therefore have to be conscious of this opportunity for movement in their designs: printed fabrics for example, while designed on paper, are rarely seen flat in use. Indeed, when used as curtains, different forms of pleating have been devised to take advantage of the aspect of surprise and change that folding gives to repeat patterns.

Textile designers and artists have been moved by the same concerns as other artists. Some work in as representational form as the limitations of the materials will allow, pressing forwards against those limitations towards more representational forms. Others have utilised the inherent qualities of the materials to portray texture, colour and pattern and to produce non-representational and abstract work of great power.

The tapestry example (opposite), which is a very old surviving example of a tapestry weaving, shows the richness that this technique can achieve. Many great artists prepared designs for tapestries. These were often in the form of full size 'cartoons'. The Victoria and Albert Museum in London has a set of seven cartoons by Raphael (1483–1520) for *The Life of Christ*. Tapestry is always made on a hand-operated loom and though the design is prepared for it, and followed closely, the hand-made qualities are an important part of the finished product.

In case you feel that this method of building up pictures line-by-line is laborious and old fashioned you might like to reflect that the computer-aided art (right) was printed in a similar, though obviously faster, way.

The most accessible textiles are available simply by buying from shops. Commercially printed textiles are available in wide varieties. Some from shops like Liberty are famous for their designs. Plain fabrics are also available in a wide variety of colours. If you start a collection, you might consider the possibility of beginning your creative work on ready-printed fabric.

Collecting and making samples are not however ends in themselves, there is no point in having the best collection if you do nothing with it. Try to collect as you work rather than wait until your collection is too extensive to manage.

Computer graphics can aid the textile designer.

Elsie Holmes, Knot Garden, *15 cm square.*

The piece above shows how the coincidence between form and content can provide an interesting image. The simple technique of a French knot has been formed into the complex shape of a knot garden. This was a formal garden whose pathways were often as complicated as a sailor's knotwork.

Try to collect examples of each of the main ways of forming or decorating fabrics. Some will be available commercially, unusual examples are worth looking out for on your travels. Some you will have to make yourself in sample form. Collecting in a systematic way will give you a bank of reference material for your later work. Interesting yarns and threads can be collected in the same way. You might like to start to collect scraps of cloth of different colours. Swatch books are a convenient way to collect printed material if you can get hold of one from the manufacturer. Polythene might be useful for collage or appliqué work.

TEXTILES

Drawing for Textiles

It is crucial that you learn to prepare your textile work properly. Though improvisation is possible, most textile forms require technical processes, in some cases more than one, and these need to be planned for. This is especially true for embroidery techniques where the developing effects of colour and texture can change the direction of a work in progress. Often techniques required can only be identified and adapted through the use of small samples.

C. Harrison Townsend, Omar, design for a silk and wool doublecloth, Victoria and Albert Museum, London.

To try the methodical approach detailed here, start by making a development sheet of your own. Choose a subject based on a photograph or series of photographs of real objects. Do not decide on a final technique to be used before you start but rather let your preparation work lead you to find techniques that will give you the effects you want.

Drawing also plays an important part in the development of a piece of work. This can be seen in carefully worked out drawings like the one above. This shows in graphic details the motif in a printed design. In the case of this drawing it was passed on to other skilled workers to be translated into a complete printed cloth. Often, the whole process takes place in the art studio in school and the student is expected to carry out *all* the functions of artist, designer and craftsperson in order to obtain a finished product. You will appreciate the need to be well organised and to plan ahead!

Drawings do not need to be as 'finished' as the one above. Sometimes they take the form of sketches which are developed through such techniques as collage samples with tissue paper to create the illusions of transparency on which some designs rely.

Gail Harker, Snow Queen Cape worksheet.

The carefully worked development sheets on this page show one artist's view of how a piece of preparatory work might develop.

In this case drawings helped the artist to select and focus on areas of particular interest. Samples and small trial pieces helped her work out just how a desired effect could be achieved. This step-by-step approach helped the artist make sense of the images she had first discovered and translate them into a finished piece. In developing an organised approach to textile work you will enhance the finished product and often find ideas, and interests, for the next piece of work you do.

If all of this sounds a rather stiff and solid way to work, perhaps devoid of the excitement and risk that some art forms enjoy, then you will soon develop a method of working of your own. This will, perhaps, take the best ideas from the method suggested above and the most effective ways that your experience tells you will work for you. Each artist needs to develop their own approach to the synthesis between ideas and techniques that are such a marked feature of textile work.

Textiles

Though the drawings by Mary Quant for dress designs are simple, they give an accurate and complete view of the garment. If you wish to use textiles for garments, especially for your own designs, then you will need to develop a style of presentation drawing that will show off your work in its best light. Your drawings must be clear and simple, without the presentation tricks that will make your work look good as a drawing but will hide and detract from the garment. Keep uppermost in your mind the thought that the garment is paramount. No amount of flashy presentation will make a poorly designed garment look good. Quite often, as in this case, the figure will be reduced to a formal shape, often only suggested. This does *not* mean that figure drawing is unimportant to the potential fashion designer. Since most of their product is ultimately going to finish up on a customer, a clear understanding of shape, size and proportions is crucial.

Below is a working drawing giving details of a pattern, its repeat, and the colours to be used. Since each colour has to be printed separately this colour separation is very important. Any drawing that goes to the manufacturers to be made into a printed textile is expected to show the full pattern and to indicate the repeat of that pattern.

Mary Quant (b.1934), three sample dress designs.

C. F. A. Voysey (1857–1941), Seagulls, 1890–91, *drawings for a wool and silk fabric, watercolour and pencil, Victoria and Albert Museum, London.*

Freelance designers present their work in this form. The two examples here are drawings prepared for commercial use. You will need to be able to present drawings like this if you wish to work commercially. They show that the artist needs to be well aware of the technical processes that will ultimately turn the artist's ideas into a finished product. You will also need to be able to produce working drawings of this type if you wish to take your own work beyond the design stage. If you intend to produce printed textiles for example, then this type of drawing will be needed to cut your stencil from. If you are block printing then your drawing will be transferred by carbon paper.

ART & DESIGN

Harry Napper (1860–1940), design developed in the manufacturer's studio, a working drawing.

Though a clear understanding of the processes involved in production is of value to the designer, sometimes it can inhibit the introduction of new ideas. In the 1930s industrial designers were felt to be failing the textiles industry. Their training and their preoccupation with avoiding technical problems led them away from individuality and imaginative design. Painters like Paul Nash (1889–1946) and Cedric Morris became involved in the work of Cresta Silks, experimenting with block printing silks. The decline of the textile industry in this country can be blamed, in part, for the lack of new and imaginative designs. Few companies like Cresta Silks or the Edinburgh Weavers were brave enough to use the art of the day for inspiration. Your own designs and fabrics will be improved by a knowledge of the techniques used to produce or print them, but you must try and avoid the trap that led industry into safe, technically sound solutions rather than bold, imaginative ones.

The working drawing (above) was developed from a design by Harry Napper in the manufacturer's studio. It has been coloured on to graph paper so that the weaving process for the fabric can be set up. The notes in the top left corner give details of the colours while the numbers along the vertical and horizontal axes count the number of threads in the warp (vertical) and the weft (horizontal). A material is woven when the threads continually cross and recross each other. Take apart a piece of woven cloth like hessian and you will see how it has been made.

Make a collection of the work of fashion designers. You can find examples of their presentation drawings in magazines like Vogue and Harpers & Queen. From the examples that you have collected and your own figure drawings try and develop a suitable style to show off your own fashion ideas.

ART & DESIGN

TEXTILES

The Work Process

WEAVING

Almost all commercially available fabrics are woven. Machines called looms produce great lengths of fabric from a variety of yarns. Fabrics can be plain or they can have the patterns woven into them. Patterned woven fabrics are usually more expensive than those that have the pattern printed on them. Weaving can produce a wide range of fabric weight, from the finest silk to heavy woven carpets depending on the yarn used.

Artists have used the technique to imaginatively weave non-textile materials, as the woven pot on the page opposite shows. Students have achieved interesting results by weaving lengths of wire. Copper wire, in a variety of different weights, can make jewellery when woven and then cut into shape. The weave can be persuaded to stay together by beating the copper on a planishing stake. Square section aluminium armature wire can also produce interesting forms when woven. Sheep hurdles are traditionally made by weaving a lattice of split chestnut sticks.

The pieces on these two pages show the wide range of materials that can be used. The heavy wall hanging (left) is woven with broad bands of highly textured, multicoloured strips. The woven structure can still be seen, creating an added dimension as light falls on the curved surfaces. In finer woven fabrics the structure is too fine to be seen, the fabric is seen to have a continuous flat surface.

The non-textile woven sculpture (above right) shows how the technique can be adapted to produce a more solid wall hanging. Several layers of wooden grids are interwoven with textured dyed threads and rags. You might like to experiment with the different types of trellis work that can be found in garden centres. This ready-made solid structure might be common to a whole group of students working on the same piece or it could provide a challenge to make each student's work different.

Interesting work can also be produced if you put part of the weaving process into reverse by selectively removing threads from a length of woven material: thread pulling. The more open work areas produced by this method could be backed by different colours or textures or the weft removed could be replaced by threads, strips of coloured rag or indeed any other flexible material. Experiment with weaving different materials. You could try non-textile materials like copper wire, metal strips, foil, wooden lathes, plants, cardboard or paper. You can also experiment with solid, inflexible materials for either the warp or the weft. Your other material will, of course be flexible and it is this that will bind the 'fabric' together. Since the machinery available in most schools limits the scale you can work to, look for ways to increase the size of your woven work. You could for example build a woven sculpture in the same way Michael Brennand-Wood has, but using carpet roll cardboard tubes as your warp.

John Hinchcliffe, woven wall hanging, 1978, 259 × 198 cm, Victoria and Albert Museum, London.

ART & DESIGN

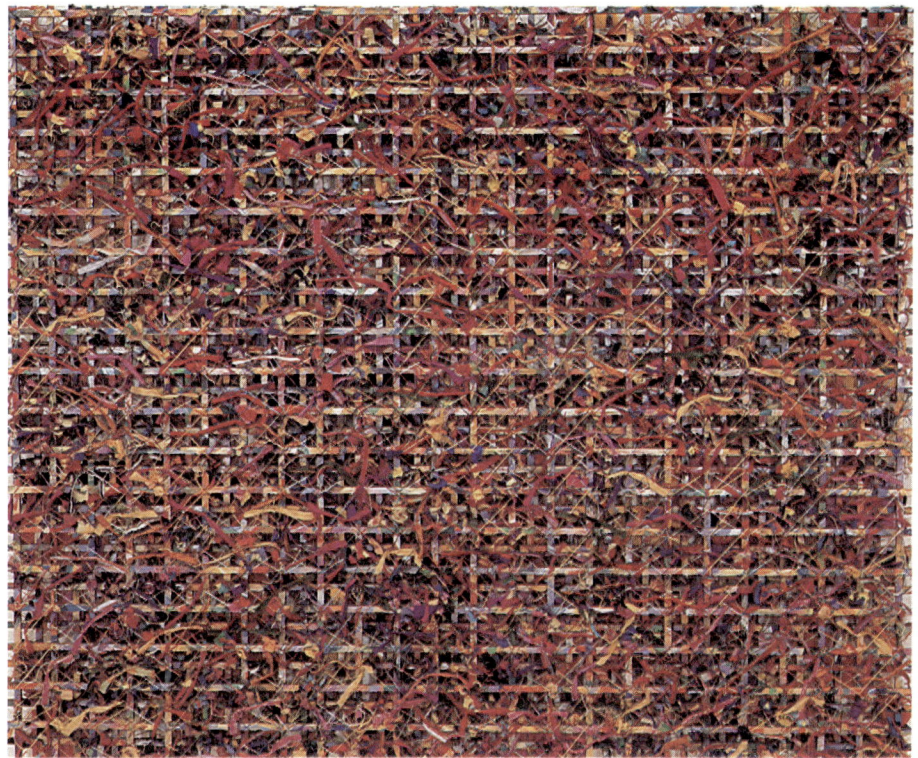

Michael Brennand-Wood (b.1952), Trailing Colours, 1983, *144 × 120 × 7 cm plaited wood mesh, threaded silks, cotton fabric and wire.*

Examine the woven clay pot below. Try to create a piece of work using a woven pliable material like clay. Experiment with the decorative effects that could be achieved by weaving different coloured clays together in this way. Woven textiles made within schools have, traditionally, been rather stiff. Narrow braid or card looms are most frequently used. These allow the school weaver to produce narrow strips suitable for belts or the facings of garments. With some of the suggestions above, and no doubt far more imaginative ones of your own, you could try to escape from this limited format.

Until the introduction of broadloom weaving in this country in the 13th century, and in many areas of the world where broadloom cloths are not made, fabrics are often made by sewing together many narrow strips of cloth. There are some particularly fine examples of this method to be found if you look at West African textiles.

Jan Schachter, woven coils, 10 × 8 × 8 cm.

ART & DESIGN 13

Textiles

APPLIQUÉ

Appliqué is a method of forming, or making, fabric surfaces by adding or 'applying' other fabrics. Fabrics are sewn into place (if they are stuck down it is called collage). It is also possible to bond fabrics together using a double-sided tape.

Pat Sales, Sunbathers, *appliqué.*

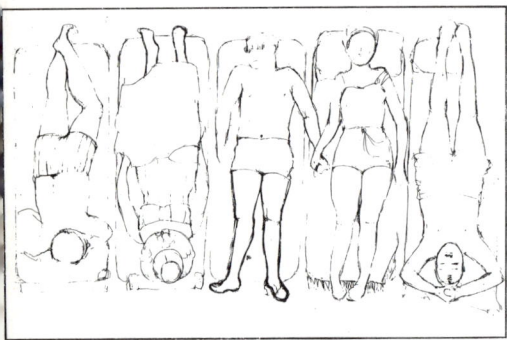

Pat Sales, Sunbathers, *preparatory drawing.*

The work above was developed from a series of drawings of people on the beach (an ideal occupation for those bored by endless sunbathing). Pat Sales then simplified her drawings until the stage above was reached. You might like to try the same subject based on drawings of your own, or you could equally well reach this stage by working from your own photographs. A simplified drawing could be made by tracing from your originals, drawing only the most important lines.

In the *Sunbathers* each figure was cut from card, covered with the material from old pairs of tights, and given form by carefully padding with wadding. Garments, towels, hats and other accessories were made from pieces in the artist's extensive collection of fabrics. The process of simplifying your originals helps to focus on the essentials of the figures' pose. As a result the figures manage to look 'real' even though the technique has obvious limits.

However, details can be added by changing the size and arrangement of the stitching. Endless lines of machine stitching can produce the nervous energy of a sketch, and still capture the immediacy of the 'frozen' moment.

14 ART & DESIGN

You might like to try the idea of a piece of work based on a group of people. Perhaps you could start by collecting photographs and drawings. Suitable subjects might be found by watching groups of students at break or lunchtime, children at play in the local park or primary school, or parents and children at the end of the day at the infants school.
All the illustrations in this section use the human figure. The limitations of the fabric technique does not allow for photographic realism. The works therefore rely on simplified form and closely observed gesture to create an illusion of reality.

Roger Mayne, Southam Street, North Kensington, London, 1956.

You could look at the way photographers have used this idea of the 'frozen' moment. This is why the camera is such a useful tool in the search for raw material for this type of work. With a camera, you can observe and record the way people behave when they are unaware of being watched. Try to be unobtrusive so that your subjects do not react to your presence. Look at the photographs of Roger Mayne to help you.

Produce a piece of work that reflects your experience of observing people. You could make a photographic record of your own. This could, with drawing, form an important part of the work process.

ART & DESIGN

TEXTILES

Form and Content

THE CONTAINER

Ann Rutherford, Little Precious, *20 cm long × 17.5 cm wide × 18 cm deep.*

The work on these two pages is important because it shows, through an experience with which we can all share, a rare coincidence between content and form.

We have all either 'cooed' over a pram ourselves or stood back, perhaps embarrassed, while others have done so. We can all therefore identify with the content of the piece. The form is that of a box or container, rather in the way that the pram is. The success of this piece is in the close correspondence between the two elements, form and content. Do you think such a close relationship between these two elements is important in a work of art?

Think of traditional uses for textiles as containers, it might help if you list them. The list will be long, from hand-bags to peg bags, from tea cosies to hats! Choose one item from your list and collect examples either from the real things or by photograph or drawing. Try to discover the reasons for its basic form.

Another view of the opposite piece.

What problems do containers set out to solve? You might like to make an in-depth study of the most imaginative, or most functional, example that you have found. Having studied the forms that already exist and the problem that your object seeks to address you are ready to start thinking of a design of your own.

Can you discover an interesting link between content and form and develop your design along these lines? Make a study of the types of soft toys that are available to very young children, and try to find out about the rules which govern the manufacture of toys for the very young. As they are mass produced they tend to be very simple and so may miss opportunities for child development. They might be more interesting for example if they contained contrasts of colour, texture and pattern.

Perhaps you could create a piece of soft sculpture which could be used as a toy and would allow a young child to experience colour, texture or pattern? It doesn't have to be made in the shape of some animal: for children without experience of the shapes of many animals, the cuddly bear shape is often totally abstract anyway.

Do you think the element of surprise is important in the work? After all, when a box is closed you can have little idea of what is in it.

ART & DESIGN 17

TEXTILES

Noel Dyrenforth, Gateway II, 1980, *calico, naphtol, stencilled, wax sprayed and pleated,* 170 × 170 cm.

DYE RESIST DECORATION

These two pages show examples of the way a traditional technique like wax resist or Batik has been developed to meet the modern artist's needs. Batik is a method used originally in the Indonesian island of Java, to colour lengths of fabric. Modern artists have used this technique as the basis for a more spontaneous art form.

Traditional Batik was often used to produce repeat patterns in a variety of natural colours. The subtle browns and creams created from natural dyes have, in some areas, given way to more garish, commercially produced dyes. The technique uses wax, applied hot to prevent the dye from reaching the fabric and so changing its colour. Successive areas are blocked out with wax so that different colours can appear on the same fabric length. The crackle effect that breaks up the waxed-over areas is caused by dye seeping through the cracks in the wax.

Wax resist is not the only form of resist possible. Dyes can be blocked out by starch. This is a common method used by the Yoruba, a group of people found on the coast of West Africa. A more accessible form of resist, for use with cold water dyes, might be margarine. This can be applied when melted by brush, and has the added advantage of being easier to brush than hot wax. The margarine can be removed with hot soapy water. Masking-tape can also be used to resist dyes. By careful control of the medium, craft, skill and a creative, rather than an imitative outlook, these two artists have produced beautiful modern textiles.

Dyed lengths of fabric can be hung as banners or flags. The movement, generated by the winds or indoor currents of air, add interest. Produce a series of light, coloured fabric flags. Perhaps you could plan a group of flags to hang together? Your flags and banners could be used to advertise a product or event. They could be used to decorate a dull space. They could be used to identify a group. Your research could examine such work as Trade Union banners, Japanese or Chinese military flags, regimental flags from local churches or even processional banners from the churches themselves. Many you will find have been coloured through embroidery and you might like to include some in your dyed designs. Take care to consider movement in your work, stirred by the breeze your flags could present an ever changing display of pattern and colour.

It is possible to apply wax to the fabric in a variety of traditional and non-traditional ways. Wax can be applied using for example an absorbent stamp, like crumpled cloth, paper towel or a soft wooden shape. It is possible to work in reverse, laying on the resist and then deliberately weakening it to allow the dye to penetrate through in some areas. Resist can also be sprayed on: try spray starches and see what sort of effects you can get with these and a simple stencil.

Experiment: don't be trapped into a method of working simply because it's traditional and therefore you know it will work. Art is about taking risks, the satisfaction when a risk succeeds is well worth the failures.

You might like to experiment with these techniques and produce some resist dyed textiles of your own. Frequently dyed fabrics are used as the backgrounds for other techniques or to be included in them, consider for example weaving with strips of Batik cloth.

Norma Starszakowna (b.1945), Rising Rune II, 1989, batiked and direct dyed silk, 53 × 60 cm.

ART & DESIGN

Textiles

PRINTED TEXTILES

The two illustrations of printed textiles shown here are examples of the work of designers better known as painters.

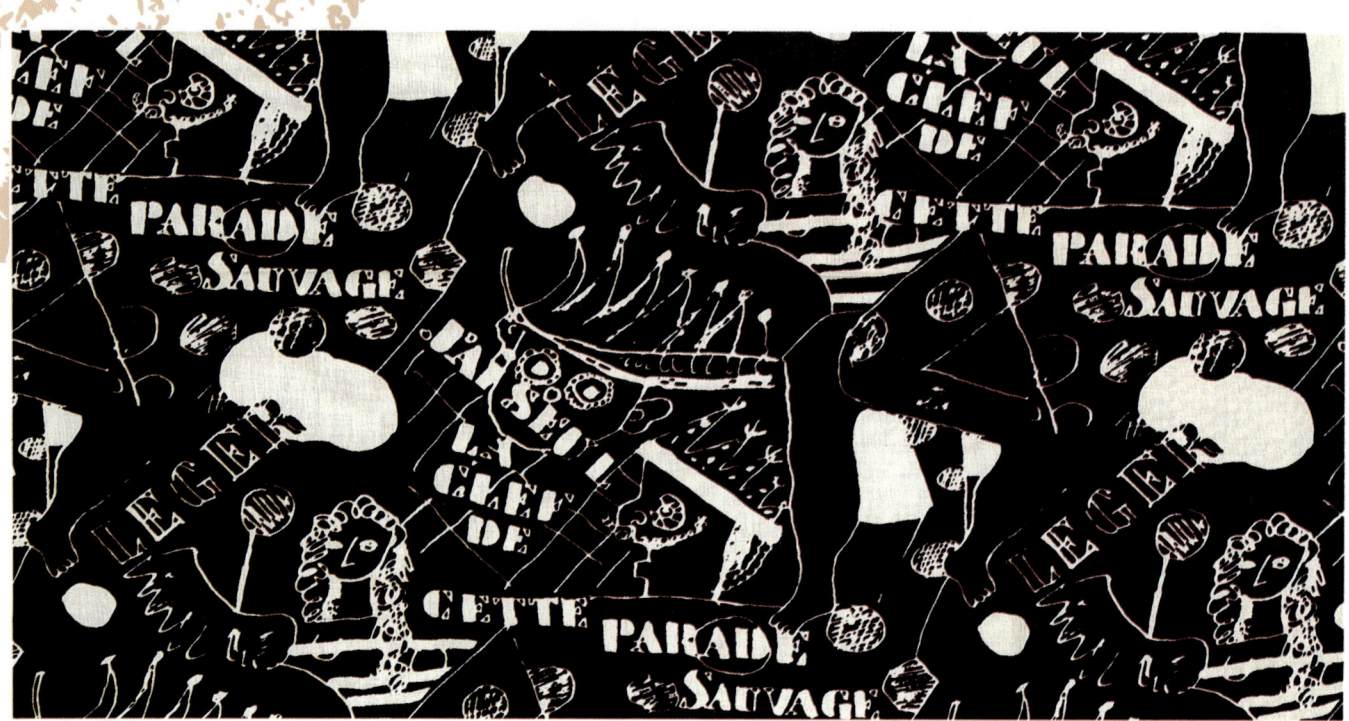

Fernand Leger (1881–1955), Parade Sauvage, *screenprinted cotton, Victoria and Albert Museum, London.*

Choose one or two of your favourite painters. Imagine the type of textiles they might have designed and the sort of materials they would have used. Work up a length or series of samples based on your ideas. If you choose an artist like Duncan Grant or Vanessa Bell you might be able to compare it with the work they actually did produce.

Raoul Dufy (1877–1953), textile design, Victoria and Albert Museum, London.

ART & DESIGN

Part of a mosaic floor from the Basilica of St Mark's, Venice, 13th century.

The 13th century mosaic from Venice demonstrates the sources of pattern that might be available to you from a study of Art History. The Renaissance flourished in Venice which was one of the most powerful states in Europe at this time, due to the influence of a closed group of aristocratic families. This meant it could attract some of the best craftsmen. Look for other examples of patterns in Art Historical material.

Artists in Britain had a long tradition of involvements in the design of textiles. In the 19th century this centred around the work of the Art and Crafts Movement led by William Morris. In the early part of this century the 'Omega' workshops were founded by Roger Fry (1866–1934).

Artists were encouraged to design everyday objects, including textiles. It was thought that introducing art into the ordinary home would raise the quality of society. Duncan Grant (1885–1978) and Vanessa Bell (1879–1961) produced successful textiles. You might find it interesting to compare the textile designs and the paintings of these two artists.

Throughout the century painters designed fabrics either for commercial or limited production. The most successful like Henri Matisse (1869–1954) and Henry Moore (1898–1987) realised the significance of the materials they worked with, creating designs that looked good folded, crumpled or rippling with movement.

Examples of the works of these artists and others can be found at the two major museums devoted to textiles. The Victoria and Albert Museum in London and the Whitworth Museum, Manchester have major collections of textiles from many cultures, techniques and periods of history.

Examine the way textiles and costumes are portrayed by painters. Looking at paintings is an unrivalled way to study how these have developed through history. Look for example at the way northern Europeans dressed at the time of the Van Eyck brothers, (late 14th to early 15th century), or you could look at how Italians dressed for their formal portraits at the hands of Bronzino (1503–1572).

ART & DESIGN

Textiles

REPEAT PATTERNS

You might like to consider why repeat patterns are used so frequently. Why can't we have patterns that vary across the entire length and width of a fabric?

C. F. A. Voysey, Let Us Prey, 1974, *design for a textile, Victoria and Albert Museum, London.*

With the introduction of computer control technology this should be possible, so are there other reasons for repeat printings? If you look at the drawing on page 8 you can see how repeat pattern designs are passed on to the printer. The pattern to be repeated is isolated but the repeat is indicated by fainter, or by outline drawing. See if you can isolate the repeated part of the pattern example above. Choose a fabric sample that contains the whole repeat and see if you can isolate that.

Design a simple repeat pattern and work up the drawings so that they could be presented to a printer as an example of your work as a freelance designer. You might be able to find out from conversation with such a designer a bit more about the way manufacturers like designs to be presented to them. You could also base your design on simple geometric shapes. As an alternative you might like to base your design around a theme, perhaps a children's nursery or hospital unit. To do this you would need a clear idea of the uses to which your fabric might be put and it could give you experience of designing for a particular, and limited, market. Try to discover how patterns are matched when, for example, two lengths of fabric are joined edge to edge to make curtains. You could discuss this with a shop that sells patterned fabrics or carpets.

ART & DESIGN

Try to make a collection of fabrics that have repeat patterns, you only need to keep enough to show the repeat. The heavy printed fabrics of the Arts and Crafts Movement, designed by such artists as William Morris (1834–1896) will require careful and thoughtful analysis for quite frequently the repeat is difficult to identify.

It might help with your design work if you set out to make a collection of patterns as they occur in nature or in the man-made world. You might start with the most obvious pattern forms, those that are regular and repeat the same simple element over and over again. You will quickly find that these are not the only patterns that repeat similar shapes in an irregular pattern, an example of this pattern might be made by the way leaves naturally fall on the grass. Even more complex patterns can be discovered if you have the patience to look for them.

Make your collection by drawing or by taking photographs. Classify your collection according to the complexity and interest of the patterns you have discovered. From your collection make up some designs to the stage that you might present them to a manufacturer as a freelance designer. Look at the way artists use repeated images in their work, an obvious example is the screenprints produced by Andy Warhol (1928–1989). Try to examine the work of other artists that use repeats in their work. Why do repeats feature in this way?

This wrapping paper (below) is a very simple repeat pattern. Its geometric design is in direct contrast with the more complex repeat opposite. Roy Lichtenstein (b. 1923), famous for his 'pop art' has created a design that fits within the mainstream of his art. He has made no concession at all to the function of this product. Do you think this design, which looks good stretched out flat, will look as good when wrapped around a package?

Do you think that designers should take into account the uses that their product might be put to even if this compromises their designs?

Patterns in nature: feathers on a duck's back.

Roy Lichtenstein (b. 1923), printed wrapping paper design, 1969, 75 cm wide.

ART & DESIGN

Textiles

Embroidery

Look at the work on these two pages; you will see some unconventional use of embroidery skills. The artists show how imaginative use of materials can revitalize traditional techniques.

The transparent background of acetate (thin plastic) means that the embroidery appears to be free-standing, unsupported by the background. This gives the piece on the left, which is a sample, an unreal quality.

You might like to look at other open fabric structures that could be embroidered on. Machine-made lace was produced in Nottingham during the later part of the 18th century until the middle of the 20th. It celebrated its break with traditional hand-made lace by incorporating non-traditional subject matter. The piece opposite was produced for the Paris Exhibition in 1900.

Try to build up a collection of this valuable material, if not through actual examples then through drawings, photographs or photograms. To create a photogram place the lace on a sheet of photographic printing paper in the darkroom, expose to light and then develop and fix in the normal way. The area covered by the lace will be unexposed and therefore appear white in the photogram. William Henry Fox Talbot (1800–1877), the pioneer photographer, made many experiments with this method and with this subject. Commercial fabric shops also sell examples of nets with complex patterns woven into them. These could be used to support embroidery, you might like to experiment by working through them with different materials. These ideas might help you escape from the preconception current that embroidery requires a solid support and a limited range of stitches.

The type of open work shown (bottom right) can be created by using a support which can then be dissolved in hot or cold water. The support has been freely machined, together with sections of other open weave fabrics like organdie and net. The support was then dissolved leaving an open, fragile, lace-like effect. The end result is a new type of fabric, it owes its construction purely to its content.

The piece of work opposite shows the complexity that can develop once the traditional ideas of embroidery on cloth have been left behind. The support in this case is a mixture of fabric, plastics and paper, machine-made lace and fabric that has been sprayed and gathered. Included in the work are the skeletons of leaves and dried hydrangea petals. The outline shape is assymetrical. The technique is following the artist's conception of the content rather than the content being adjusted to fit the pre-determined size and shape of the support. In this there is a lesson for all artists; how often do we start a piece of work on a support that is sized and shaped by the packet it comes in rather than any need?

In Chris Cooke's work the assymetrical edges have the same feel as the subject she has pursued. In this piece there is a correspondence between content, the garden, and form, the final shape. To achieve this, a knowledge of content is essential. She has developed this through sketchbooks and drawings. You might feel that a sketchbook would give you the knowledge that such work requires.

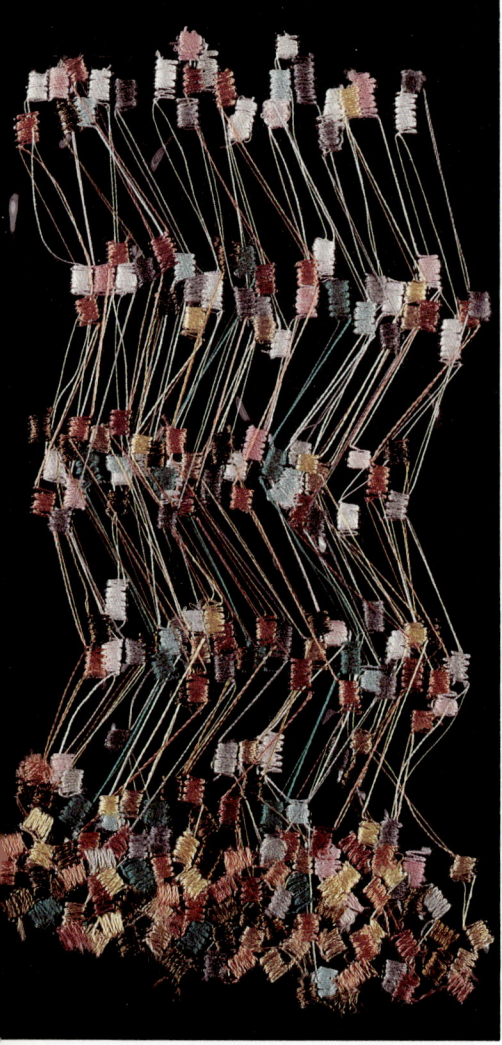

Dorothy Walker, a sample stitched onto acetate, 11.5 × 23 cm, Embroiders' Guild Collection.

24 ART & DESIGN

W. Morley, silk and cotton lace, 1900, Museum of Costume and Textiles, Nottingham.

You might like to investigate the uses of various other unconventional supports. Look at the use of theatrical coloured gel for example or clear polythene. You might like to look at the possibilities of working on clear plastic bags.
There are many other materials that you could use to produce a series of samples based on your use of unusual supports. Develop the most successful material you have found into a piece of work to be strongly lit from behind.

Chris Cooke, Winter Garden, machine-made fabrics and lace, plastics, papers, and sprayed, gathered fabric.

ART & DESIGN

Textiles

Faces

The two pieces of work illustrated on these two pages show how the flexibility of textiles can be developed into three dimensions. The quilting of the face below and the life-size character heads opposite show how the qualities of textiles can create highly individual three-dimensional work.

Characterisation like those here is often based on detailed observation over a long period of time. In the case of these works the artists clearly knew the people, or the type of person they were seeking to portray.

Audrey Ormrod, Old Woman.

26 ART & DESIGN

Renate Meyer (b. 1930),
Grandmother and Grandfather.

Examine the techniques used in these two pieces. Though the creation of work like this is complex and time consuming the techniques are capable of portraying the subject with accuracy and charm. You might like to develop one of these methods to produce a self-portrait or perhaps the portrait of someone you know well.

To work fully in the round, as in the heads above, is clearly a lengthy business. You might therefore have to restrict your work to half size but aim to keep as much of the character as you can. Your work will have to begin with drawn and photographed studies. These are better collected over a period of time and in different conditions. In this way you will, perhaps, avoid the temptation to portray a single drawing or photograph but rather try to create a synthesis of all your studies. Over a period of time you will get used to your subject and your subject will not feel they have to create an impression on you and will therefore relax. You will also need to experiment with ways of creating clothing and special effects, like skin texture and hair. For this you will need to try out your work through samples. You might also like to keep notes of conversations or even tapes so that everyone can share in the real life of the character you portray. Your best work will probably be based on a real character so do not feel tempted to work from a single photograph or drawing, you need to know the person well. You might be best advised to choose someone from inside your family or a friendly neighbour who has the patience to help you.

If you work with people you do not know or from photographs from magazines or books, you will have to guard against producing faces that, while being anatomically accurate, lack character. This changes the work from that of a person to a 'type' and with this change you lose many of the qualities that enhance the use of textiles in this way.

This method of building up an all-round picture of your subject before you start work can be used in all your art work. Work with textiles is particularly difficult because it can take so long and can be so expensive. If you prepare your work in this way you will develop a commitment to your work and to your subject which will help sustain your interest until the work is finished.

Textiles

Textiles in Three Dimensions

Maret Oppenheim is a Swiss artist. At one time she worked with a group of artists who became known as the Surrealists. The direct contrast between content and form, the impossibility of the subject being constructed and used in this fashion is characteristic of some of the work of this group. The *Lobster Telephone* in the Tate Gallery, Liverpool by Marcel Duchamp (1887–1968) creates the same impression, making us look anew at a once familiar object suddenly become strange. It is hard to fit this work within our preconceptions of the art of the 1930s and it shows how 'vintage' some 'modern' art really is.

You might like to experiment with creating a similar contrast between content and form. Use textiles to create three-dimensional objects, setting up this conflict that makes us examine the familiar again. Consider the idea of a brocade football, or look for objects that you know to be solid but can be constructed out of soft materials. Sculptors very often use the opposite point of departure.

Working with textiles can be just as challenging, if not more so, than working with other art materials if you are prepared to work with an open mind. Often the challenge, and interest, is diluted by a slavish search for technical excellence. Skills can be perfected through practice but students will only practice if they enjoy the task set, and can visualise an end product.

Maret Oppenheim (b. 1913), Object – Fur covered tea cup, saucer and spoon, 23.7 × 7.3 cm, Museum of Modern Art, New York.

Student's work, Concrete Teddy Bear.

If you are forced to produce endless samples out of the context provided by creative work you will rarely have the interest or stamina to create work of your own. In creative work with textiles, as with any other craft, sustaining interest through original work will achieve more in the long run than perfection in skills.

Try to obtain small figures and experiment with their dress. You can be as outrageous as you like. Dress your figures in the kind of outlandish wear that you might like but wouldn't dare wear yourself. Be as creative as you like, using different textile and non-textile materials. Do not think of your work as dressing a doll, you are creating a piece of sculpture.

Throughout the whole of this book the place of textiles within the sphere of Art and Design has been stressed. Textile artists have developed their work naturally in this direction. The idea of textiles as an activity that relies on craft skills rather than imagination and creativity seems to have passed away of its own accord. The division between a fabric (canvas) that is coloured by paint and one that is coloured by any of the techniques mentioned here has become redundant.

It would be quite wrong to suppose that skills are unimportant, if they were to disappear it would be a tragedy. Artists and students that take their work seriously rightly value their skills. For the student, to spend time acquiring technical excellence without the opportunity to exercise it, seems a waste of time. Textiles require a vast range of technical skills and these may require the dedication and commitment that is not present in most students.

Students need encouragement and the chance to achieve success and to learn the skills, in context, at the same time. If by the tasks set here success is possible then hopefully the motivation to improve skills will follow.

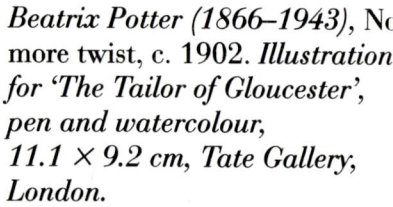

NETWORK

Beatrix Potter (1866–1943), No more twist, *c. 1902. Illustration for 'The Tailor of Gloucester', pen and watercolour, 11.1 × 9.2 cm, Tate Gallery, London.*

Look at the way artists draw or paint textiles in their pictures. Some artists specialised in the way they painted rich textiles. Look at the silver cloth of Girolamo Savoldo (active 1508–1548) in his painting *Saint Mary Magdalen approaching the Sepulchre* in the National Gallery.

THREE DIMENSIONAL AND MIXED MEDIA WORK

Look at the way textiles are used in modern mixed media work. If you look at sculptors who use textiles, Joseph Beuys (1921–1986), Robert Morris (b. 1931) and Barry Flanagan (b. 1941), you will see they have all used textiles in very different ways.

WOVEN TEXTILES

Look at commercial woven products. Try to collect as many examples as possible in as wide a range of weights as possible. Look at examples of work on simple looms—even card looms can produce interesting work if approached with imagination. Look at tapestries, both old and modern. The V&A in London has an excellent collection of hunting tapestries. For foreign travellers try the Tapestry Museum in Angers, France which houses arguably the best tapestries in the world. Country houses are a rich source of examples of woven textiles. Hardwick Hall in Derbyshire has some excellent examples. Find out about local houses that might have collections of textiles. The National Trust may be able to help.

EMBROIDERY

Look at traditional uses of embroidery—*The Bayeux Tapestry* is actually an embroidery. 'English work' was world famous during the Middle Ages for the quality of church embroidery. The Syon Cope is an example. Look at church vestments in your local church or cathedral. Many local churches have groups of workers who regularly add to the churches' embroidery collections. See if you can invite some of these groups to bring into school examples of their work. Slide loans of textiles, not only embroideries, can be arranged through The Design Council or The Crafts Council, both based in London.

PRINTING

Collect examples of printed fabrics. Find out about the different uses to which fabrics are put and how this might affect the patterns. Find out about the ways industry prints lengths of fabric. Visit the haberdashery departments in shops like Liberty's or Laura Ashley to examine the range of printed textiles they produce. The William Morris Gallery in Walthamstow is worth a visit, here you can see printed textiles from the Arts and Crafts Movement. Look for examples of Indian prints, you will often find them in Ethnographic collections like the Horniman Museum in London.

Textiles are still printed by hand using wooden blocks to this day in some parts of India. Try to find examples of hand printed textiles in the shops or markets.

RESIST DYES

Look for examples of work from other cultures, such as Batik from Java or starch resist from the Yoruba areas of Nigeria. You may be able to find out more about techniques used by other cultures from the Museum of Mankind in London. By looking at examples of dyes in use, can you find examples of tie dyes used commercially? Find out about natural dyes and how they can be made. Experiment with discharge work on hand dyed or commercially dyed products. Dip-dye cloth so that you can have a wide range of colours as raw material for work in other media.

For Dianne and Serena.

ACKNOWLEDGEMENTS

Cover and title page illustration: Painted cloth depicting action at the Battle of Little Bighorn fought on June 25th 1876, probably Sioux, late nineteenth century, 216 × 89 cm, courtesy of the Department of Anthropology, Smithsonian Institution, Washington D. C., catalogue number 358425.

Special thanks are due to the following artists featured in this book who provided photographs of their work and permission to reproduce them:

Curtis and Suzanne Benzle (5 top right), Michael Brennand-Wood (13 top), Noel Dyrenforth (18), Renate Meyer (27), Audrey Ormrod (26), Jennie Parry (5 left), Ann Rutherford (16, 17), Patricia Sales (14 both), Jan Schachter (13 bottom), Norma Starszakowna (19), and students of Homewood School (2, 3, 5 bottom right, 29).

The author and publishers would like to thank the following individuals, institutions and companies who have given permission to reproduce the other photographs in this book. Every effort has been made to trace and acknowledge ownership of copyright. The publishers would be glad to make suitable arrangements with any copyright holder whom it has not been possible to contact.

Batsford (25 bottom); BT Batsford Ltd, from *Embroidery in Miniature* by Jean Brown (7 bottom); Bridgeman Art Library (8, 21); Eileen Tweedy Photography (16, 17); Embroiderers' Guild Museum Collection, Photography: Joss Revir Bany (24); © Frederick Warne and Co., 1903, 1987 (30); GDN Associates, Hastings (7 right); Glasgow Museums: The Burrell Collection, Glasgow (6); Mary Evans/Roger Mayne (15); Mary Quant Ltd (10 left); Merehurst Publishers, taken from the book *Embroidery Skills: Machine Embroidery* by Gail Harker (9); Museum of Costume & Textiles, Nottingham (25 top); Museum of Modern Art, New York © DACS 1995 (28); Roy Lichtenstein © Roy Lichtenstein/DACS 1995; Victoria and Albert Museum, courtesy of the trustees of the V&A/Daniel McGrath © ADAGP/SPADEM, Paris and DACS, London 1995 (20 top), © DACS 1995 (20 bottom).

British Library Cataloguing in Publication Data

Dunn, Chris
  Textiles. – (Art & Design Series)
  I. Title II. Series
  746

ISBN 0 340 62725 5

First published 1995
Impression number 10 9 8 7 6 5 4 3 2 1
Year 1998 1997 1996 1995

Copyright © 1995 Chris Dunn

All rights reserved. No part of this publication may be reproduced or transmitted in any form or by any means, electronic or mechanical, including photocopy, recording, or any information storage and retrieval systems, without permission in writing from the publisher or under licence from the Copyright Licensing Agency Limited. Further details of such licences (for reprographic reproduction) may be obtained from the Copyright Licensing Agency Limited, of 90 Tottenham Court Road, London W1P 9HE.

Typeset by Wearset, Boldon, Tyne and Wear.
Printed in Great Britain for Hodder & Stoughton Educational, a division of Hodder Headline Plc, 338 Euston Road, London NW1 3BH by Cambus Litho Ltd, East Kilbride.